Love.
Charlie

Happy in Soul
A Very Special Prayer for Peace

Blessed are the peacemakers,
for they shall be called children of God.
Matthew 5:9

Happy In Soul—A Very Special Prayer for Peace

For information contact:
Jannirose JOY, LLC
www.JanniroseJOY.com

First Edition

Cover design by Gaelyn Larrick

Photo Credits: By permission page 4, Cerena Mary Lauren. All others through Dreamstime.com:
9, Vitalinko; 11, Silent47; 13, Katrina Brown; 15, Denyskuvaiev; 17, Michael Elliott; 19, Pavla Zakova;
21, Landd09; 23, Pertusinas; 25, Starblue; 27, Sandor Kacso; 29, Franz Pfluegl; 31, Nikolay Mamluke;
33, Pbclub; 35, Irina Veremeenko; 37, Kenishirotie; 39, Radim Spitzer; 41, Itzhaki;
43, Patryk Kosmider; 45, Serban Enache; 47, Anke Van Wyk.

ISBN: 978-1-4675-6545-5

13 14 15 16 17   10 9 8 7 6 5 4 3 2 1

Happy in Soul
A Very Special Prayer for Peace

by Charlie Fenimore
with Jannirose JOY Fenimore

Published by
Bright Morning Star Creations
Jannirose JOY LLC
Yellow Springs, Ohio

Dedication

To my heart friend James:

I am glad to be a peace man with you in happiness. We are helping God shine life and love and joy to our world.

Thank you for seeing my light with your spiritness.

Love from your friend,

Charlie

Foreword

Questions by Jannirose
Answers by Charlie

Charlie, why did you want to write a book?
For the hearts to shine with loving brightness and soulness.

How do you think it will help people?
To bring hope for them in their hearts.

What is your wish for the world?
Our souls with God and greatness for all spirits.

How do you hope your prayer will touch people?
Feeling love and brightness to angels and joyness for everyone.

Introduction

It brings me joy to introduce my son, Charlie Fenimore, with whom my husband and I were blessed almost twenty years ago through the miracle of adoption. Charlie was born in the summer of 1993 with the added bonus of Down syndrome, which we soon realized made him very interesting to know and love.

When he was just a small child, it became clear he could touch hearts with the accuracy of a surgical laser. After many years of observing him and his peers with Down syndrome, I've concluded this ability is encoded on the extra chromosome required for membership in this very special population.

As our son grew into adolescence, his keen sensitivity revealed itself in a rather extraordinary way. At around the age of thirteen, Charlie's gifts began to emerge in the form of what he called "prayers." The first one, featured in a weekly column I wrote for a Texas newspaper, was received by readers with genuine enthusiasm. Since then, we've accumulated a large body of such prayers that he dictates to me, and I transcribe, when the words rise into his awareness from the depths of his soul.

There's a wide range in the style Charlie uses for his prayers, depending on the circumstances. Sometimes he speaks in short phrases, and other times his messages come through in complete sentences. Often, his words paint a subtle, impressionistic picture that invites deeper contemplation. But on occasion, he delivers a line or two so stunningly clear that I'm certain he has a direct connection to the Divine.

I believe Charlie's abilities are similar to those of wise ones from other times and places. Many with the gift of spiritual insight receive wisdom that belies their normal state of understanding. It's the same with Charlie. When I read his prayers to him some time after he's received them, he normally doesn't recognize them as his own; but once I remind him that he's the author of those beautiful, heartfelt words, he reacts with sheer delight.

I recall the year he made a birthday prayer for a friend of ours, but when the special day arrived, I couldn't find it. A little sheepishly, I asked Charlie to do it again, and he politely obliged. Soon after he'd dictated the new one, the original surfaced, and I was surprised to discover the two prayers were almost identical in wording. This experience gave me the confirmation that there's something much grander at work in the delivery of his inspired messages.

One of his favorite times to "do a prayer," as he says, is when we're waiting to be served at a restaurant. These are the moments when his messages are conveyed in a shorter, simpler form. But in the times when there are no distractions or when the need is great, his prayers can be so exquisitely worded they leave me in breathless silence, reveling in the profound wisdom that comes through our everyday angel.

Once in a while, we meet a person who doubts Charlie has the capacity for the sophisticated language he sometimes uses in his creations. Whenever he detects he's being tested, he disengages and becomes very quiet—as if to protect the treasures that are born from the wellspring of his heart. For one so young, he's a man of principle who won't be challenged by the occasional unbeliever who questions his abilities.

A few times, I've overheard someone asking him, "Who writes your prayers?" His response is always the same as he innocently answers, "My mom." Because he's very literal in his understanding, he's honestly saying that I write his words as he speaks them.

Charlie and I make a good team. I'm honored to be a messenger for one of God's special angels. I've been entrusted by Spirit to help my son touch the world with the love that flows through his heart with blessed abandon.

It may be obvious to readers that Charlie relies on a small handful of words and even invents some of his own. In my experience, he's like a fine silver flute that sings just a few pure notes to heavenly perfection. Although he rarely plays the same tune twice, there are definite themes to his arrangements.

You hold in your hands the delicate fruits of a young man's heart. My wish is that you're touched in some personal way by their essence. May you be reminded of the truth and beauty of life as you savor these gentle phrases. In the reflection of Charlie's prayer, may you remember what it means to be, as he says, "happy in soul."

JANNIROSE JOY FENIMORE
FELLOW LOVE AMBASSADOR AND PEACE MINISTER
CHARLIE'S MOTHER

Happiness is the soul of the world.

We see our whole planet in light
and feeling hearts are healed.

It is peaceful to be loved
in the sky with angels bringing hope.

Joyful and grateful are healing at home in the brightful glory.

Holiness is for everybody
and someone.

Dreaming about peace and forgiving,
the sunlight will shine to our smiles.

Open our hearts with loving joyness
and fill our days with gladness.

God brings light to our hands
and angels help us heal.

Feel the sadness, madness and loneliness with our love for the freedom.

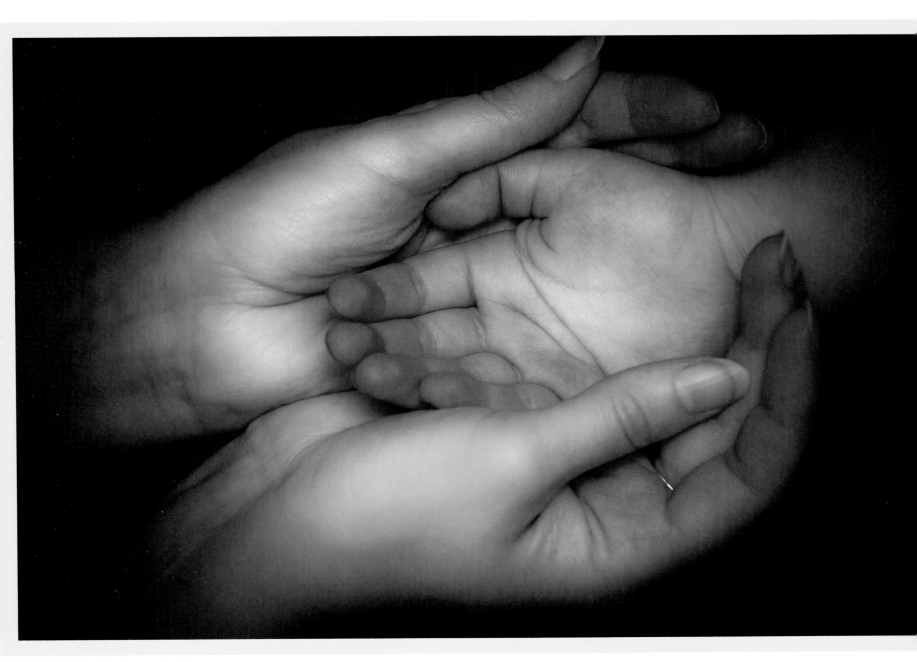

Healness is to be holy
and helpful with heartness.

We must make a change to our souls
and love people with kind relationships.

Spiritness is kindness.
Everyone must make this understanding.

The light is like bright yellow stars
and heaven is our shining joy.

We can feel this life
with our peaceful thoughts
to living love.

Forgiveness
is for human beings of the sun
to be truthful.

Spirit of love
and grateful around the light
makes everybody happy in soul.

Joy is our hopeful
and suffering in all spirits
will be healed.

Bright shining stars
about the sun of happiness
make us free inside our hearts.

Our spiritness of graceful loving
will help the world live.

Afterword

Questions by Jannirose
Answers by Charlie

What was it like for you to write this book, Charlie?
Bringing joy to make healing for souls.

Tell me what peace means to you:
Forgiveness to all hearts and joyful light around us.

Do you believe peace is possible in our world today?
We can bring peace when we remember the sun from holiness.

Where do we find the holy sun?
Angels help us to happiness and spiritness with God will be wonderness to our eyes.

Appreciation

To my family, friends, teachers,
and everybody who loves me:

You make my joy with greatness everyday.
You are special to me and your kindness
with loving in life makes me shining bright.

Thanks to Grandma and both Grandads
and my friend Jinna for your helping hearts.

Love,

Charlie

Also from Jannirose and Charlie:

Loving Outside the Lines: Lessons from an Earth Angel offers an intimate look at the lessons in love that Jannirose learns from Charlie. This book features a series of vignettes as seen through one mother's eyes describing the little miracles that unfold as her differently-abled son embraces each day with his wide-open heart.

Please visit us at
www.JanniroseJOY.com